We hope you enjoy this book.
Please return or renew it by the due date.
You can renew it at **www.norfolk.gov.uk/libraries**
or by using our free library app. Otherwise you can
phone **0344 800 8020** - please have your library
card and pin ready.
You can sign up for email reminders too.

YPS/PC

PLAYGROUP COLLECTION

D0525099

Coral Reefs

Thea Feldman

KINGFISHER

J577.78

KINGFISHER

First published 2012 by Kingfisher
an imprint of Macmillan Children's Books
a division of Macmillan Publishers Limited
20 New Wharf Road, London N1 9RR
Basingstoke and Oxford
Associated companies throughout the world
www.panmacmillan.com

Series editor: Heather Morris
Literacy consultant: Hilary Horton

ISBN: 978-0-7534-3313-3
Copyright © Macmillan Publishers Ltd 2012

All rights reserved. No part of this publication may
be reproduced, stored in or introduced into a retrieval
system, or transmitted, in any form or by any means
(electronic, mechanical, photocopying, recording or
otherwise), without the prior written permission of
the publisher. Any person who does any unauthorized
act in relation to this publication maybe liable to
criminal prosecution and civil claims for damages.

9 8 7 6 5 4 3 2 1

1TR/1011/WKT/UNTD/105MA

A CIP catalogue record for this book is available from the British Library.

Printed in China

This book is sold subject to the condition that it shall not, by way of trade
or otherwise, be lent, resold, hired out, or otherwise circulated without
the publisher's prior consent in any form of binding or cover other than
that in which it is published and without a similar condition including
this condition being imposed on the subsequent purchaser.

Picture credits
The Publisher would like to thank the following for permission to reproduce their material. Every care has
been taken to trace copyright holders. However, if there have been unintentional omissions or failure to trace
copyright holders, we apologize and will, if informed, endeavour to make corrections in any future edition.
Top = t; Bottom = b; Centre = c; Left = l; Right = r
Cover Shutterstock (SS)/tubuceo & bernd.neeser; Pages 3 Frank Lane Picture Agency (FLPA)/R. Dirscherl;
4–5 Photolibrary/Peter Arnold Images; 5 FLPA/Norbert Wu/Minden; 6t FLPA/Chris Newbert/Minden; 6b Corbis/
Brandon Cole; 7t Getty/Science Faction; 7b Alamy/Cristiano Burmester; 8t Corbis/Robert Yin; 8b Getty/Science
Faction; 9t Getty/Ken Lucas; 9b Photolibrary/Waterframe Underwater Images; 10 SS/bunpot; 11 Alamy/Steve
Bloom Images; 12t Alamy/Jane Gould; 12b Getty/Comstock Images; 13t SS/Vlad61; 13b SS/marro31;
14t Photolibrary/Imagebroker; 14b Alamy/Amar & Isabelle Guillen; 15t Photolibrary/Ross Armstrong;
15b Photolibrary/Waterframe Underwater Images; 16 FLPA/Norbert Probst; 17 SS/Ian Scott; 18 Photolibrary/
OSF; 19 Alamy/Satish Arikkath; 20 Photolibrary/Pacific Stock; 21t Photolibrary/Datacraft; 21c Photolibrary/
Bios; 21b Photolibrary/Animals Animals; 22 SS/Brian Lasenby; 23 SS/R Gombarik; 24 SS/John A. Anderson;
25 Photolibrary/Waterframe Underwater Images; 26 Alamy/Bruce Coleman Inc; 27 Corbis/Carole
Valkenier/All Canada Photos; 28–29 SS/cbpix; 30–31 Photolibrary/OSF.

Welcome to a coral **reef**!

It is the most colourful place in the sea.

Look at all the **coral**.

Coral grows in many sizes, shapes and colours.

It can look like a rock.

It can look like a plant.

But it is made of many tiny animals that grow connected to one another.

Some coral is called hard coral.

There are many kinds
of hard coral.

Some coral is called soft coral.

There are many kinds
of soft coral.

9

Look at all the coral reef fish!

There are thousands
of different kinds.

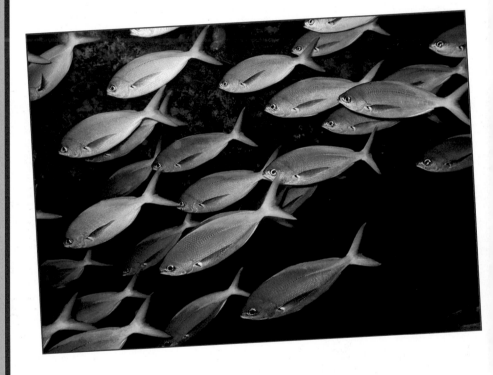

Some fish are one bright colour.

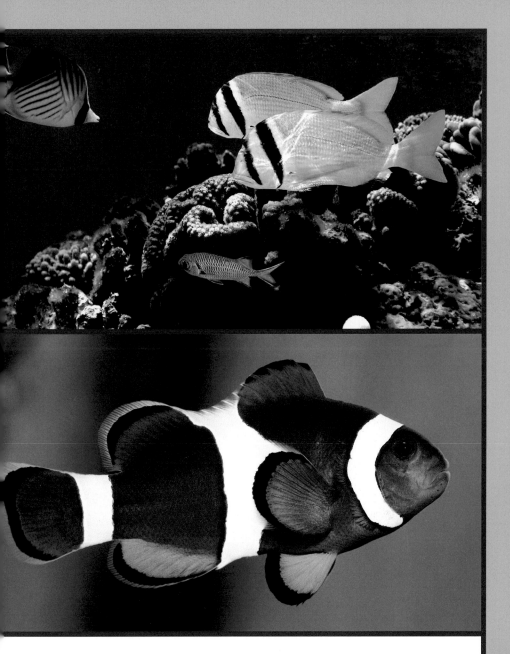

Some fish are more than
one colour.

Some fish have stripes.

Some fish have spots.

Did you know that some sharks live on coral reefs?

Sharks are fish too.

Sea horses are coral
reef fish too.

So are **sea dragons**.

Many other animals live on
coral reefs.

In the daytime,
green turtles swim.

Sea cucumbers crawl.

Starfish move on the reef.

Giant clams stay still.

Eels are fish that come out
only at night.

Some kinds of crab come out
at night too.

Sponges are animals that look like plants.

Sea grass is a coral reef plant.

Sea anemones are animals that look like flowers.

They sting fish with poison. Then they eat the fish.

Is this **clown fish** in danger?

No. The sea anemone's poison
cannot hurt the clown fish.

A clown fish can live
in a sea anemone!

So many amazing animals live in colourful coral reefs.

Let's keep coral reefs safe.

The animals are counting
on us!

Glossary

clown fish a colorful coral reef fish that can live in a sea anemone

coral many tiny sea animals that grow together as one animal at a reef

reef a mass of coral growing together under the sea

sea anemone a coral reef animal that looks like a flower

sea cucumber an animal that crawls on a coral reef

sea dragon a kind of coral reef fish

sea horse a kind of coral reef fish

sponges coral reef animals that look like plants